POOPING CATS

A Funny and Inappropriate Humping Coloring Book for those with a Rude Sense of Humor

Copyright 2019 Just 4 Jokes Coloring Books. All Rights Reserved.

ISBN: 9781670344861

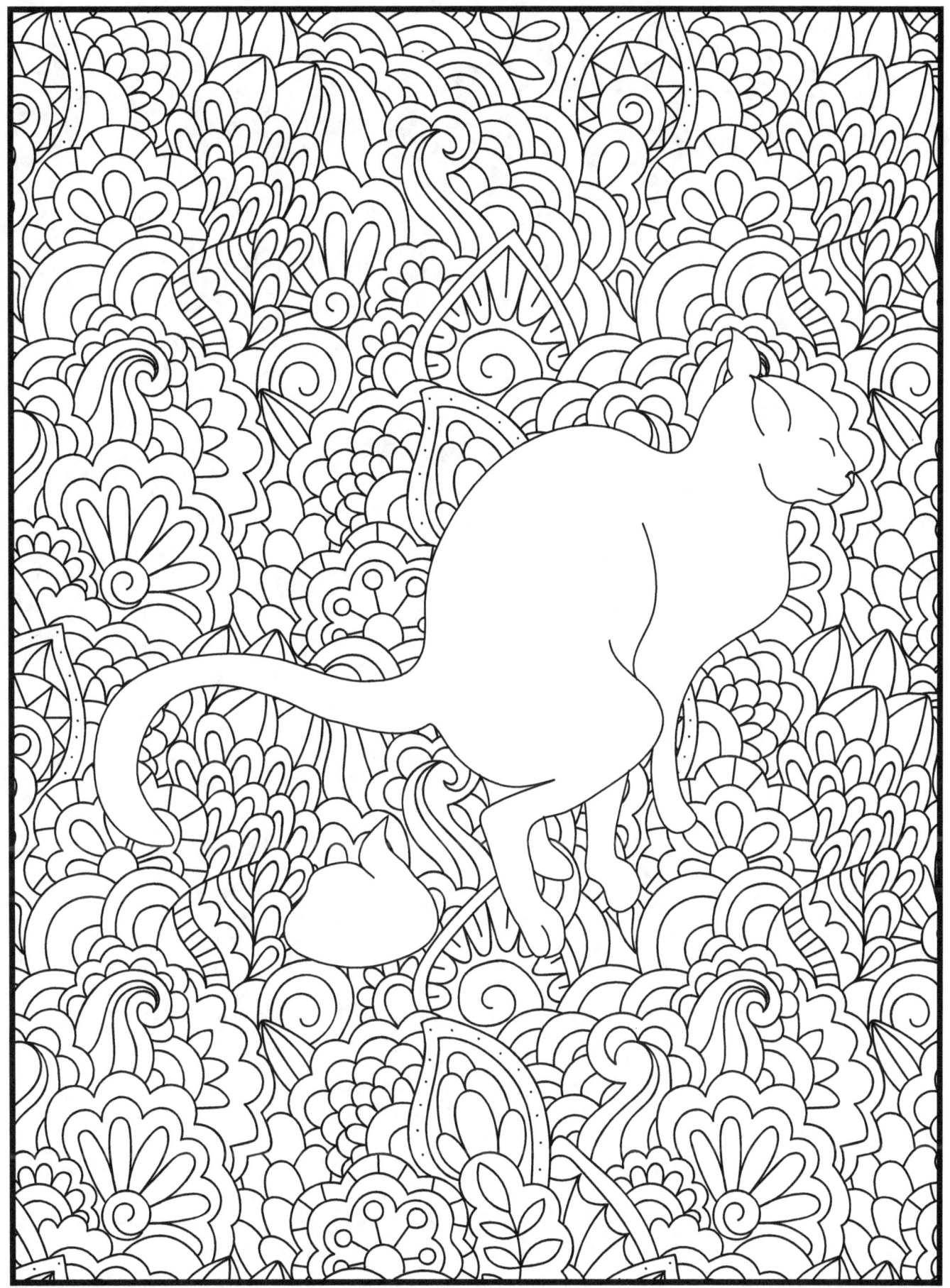

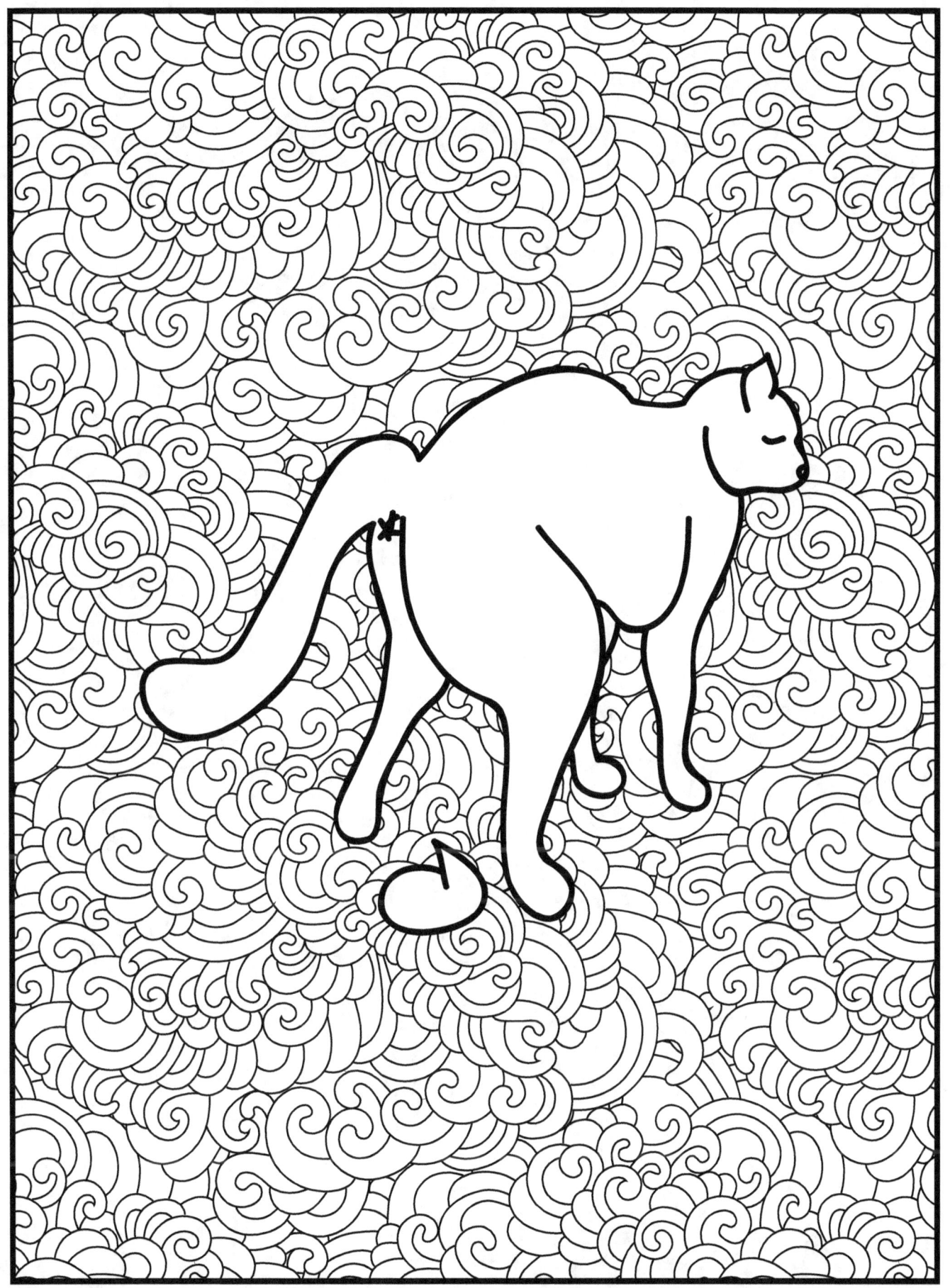

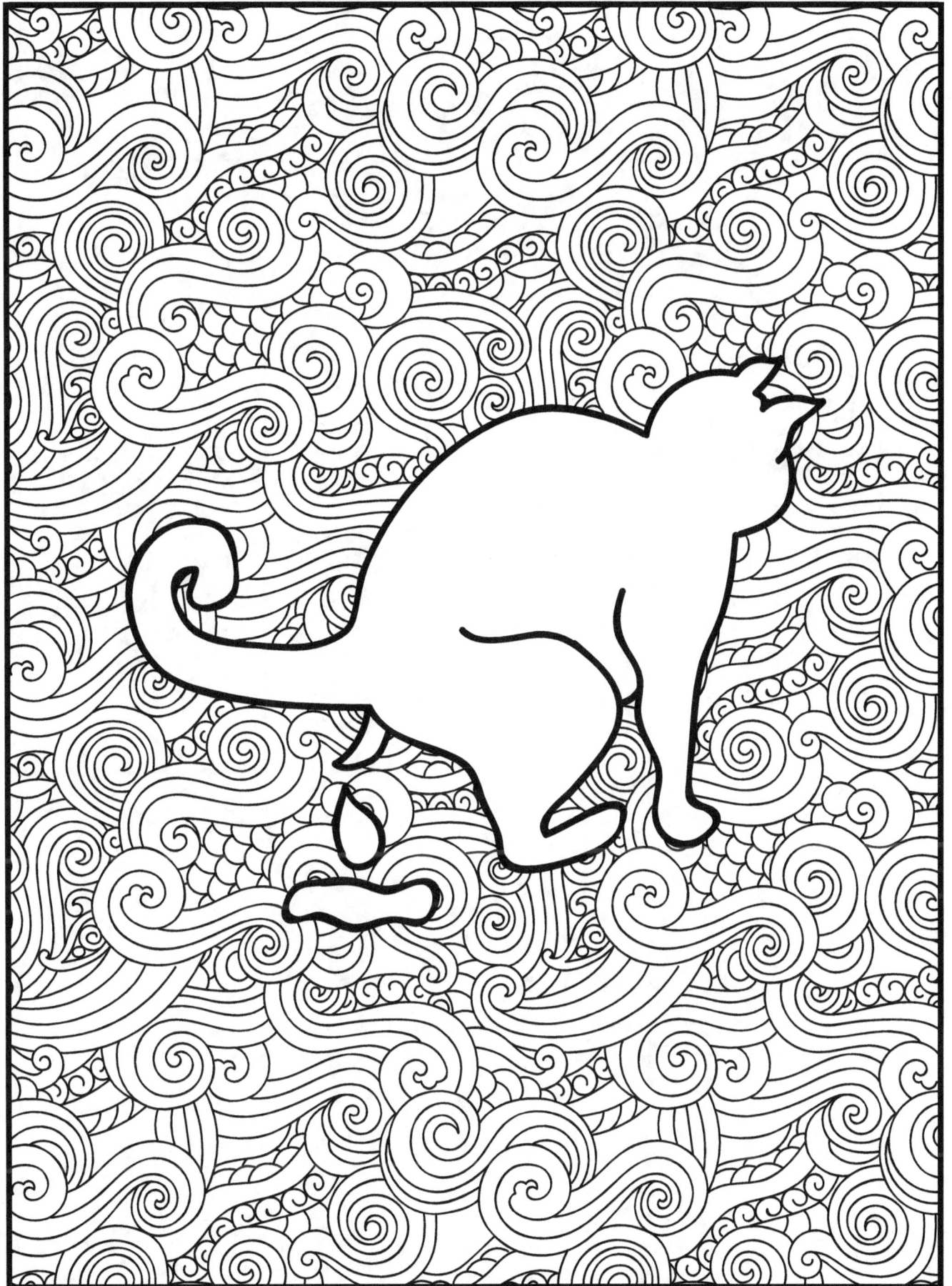

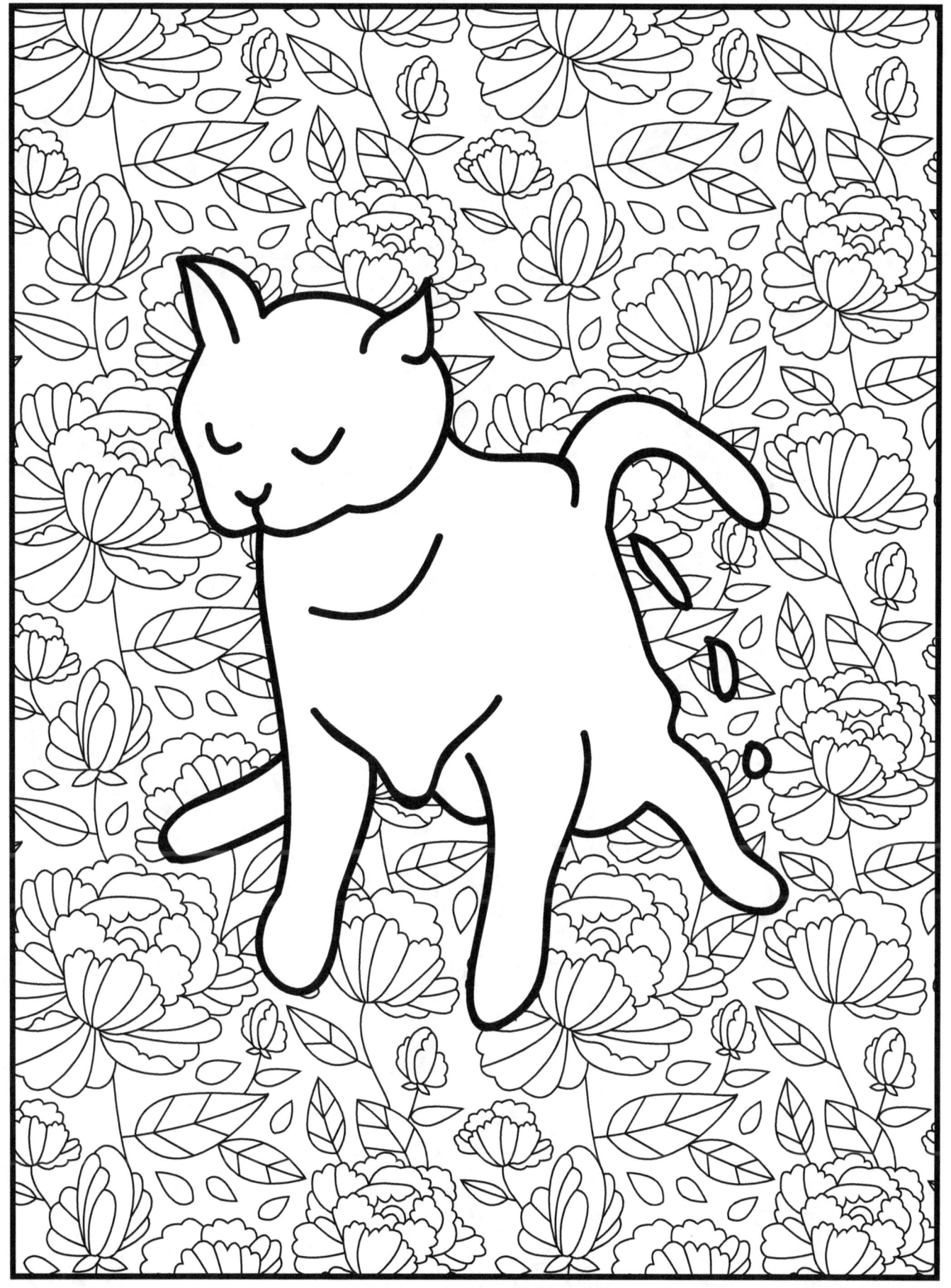

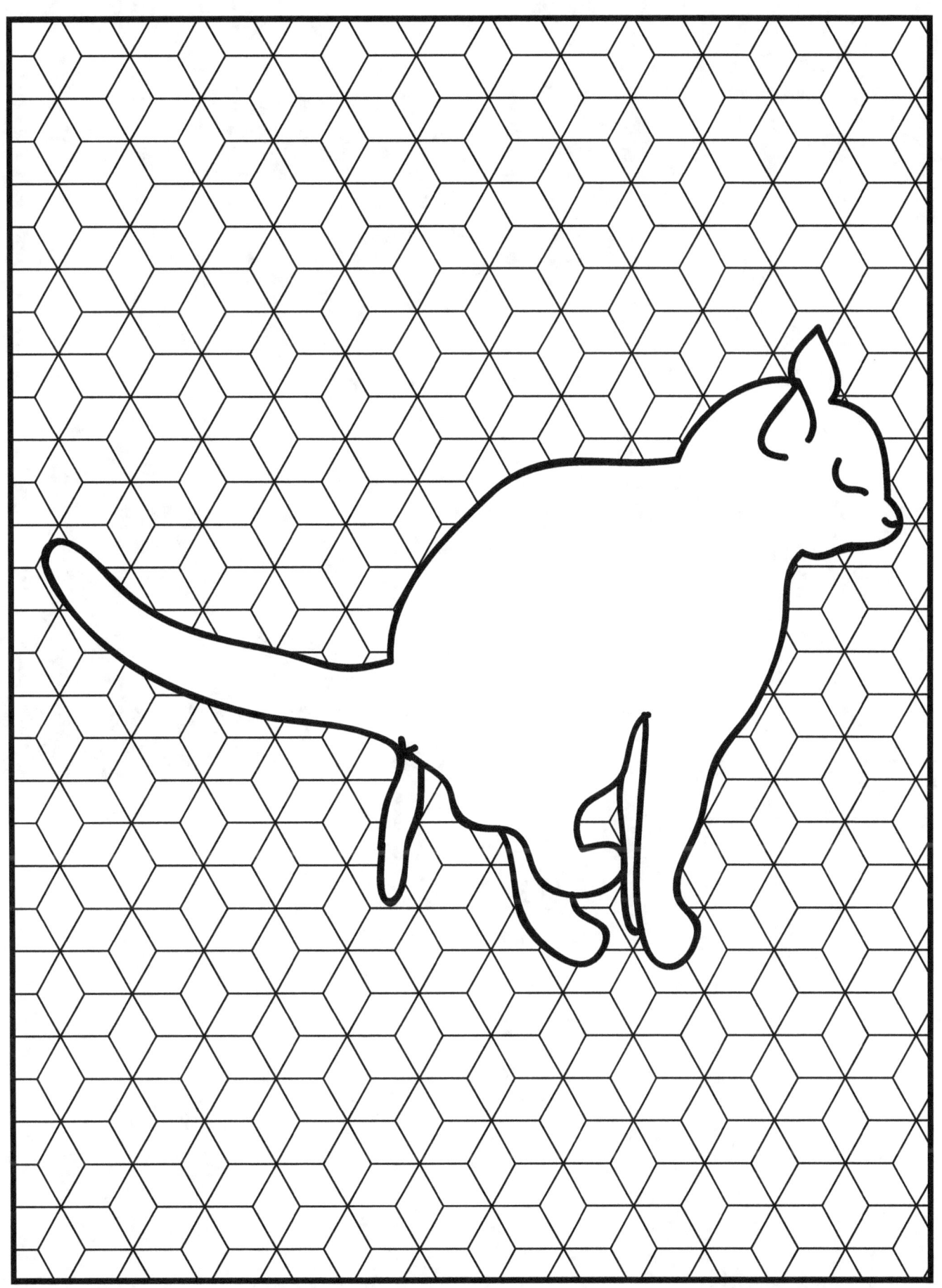

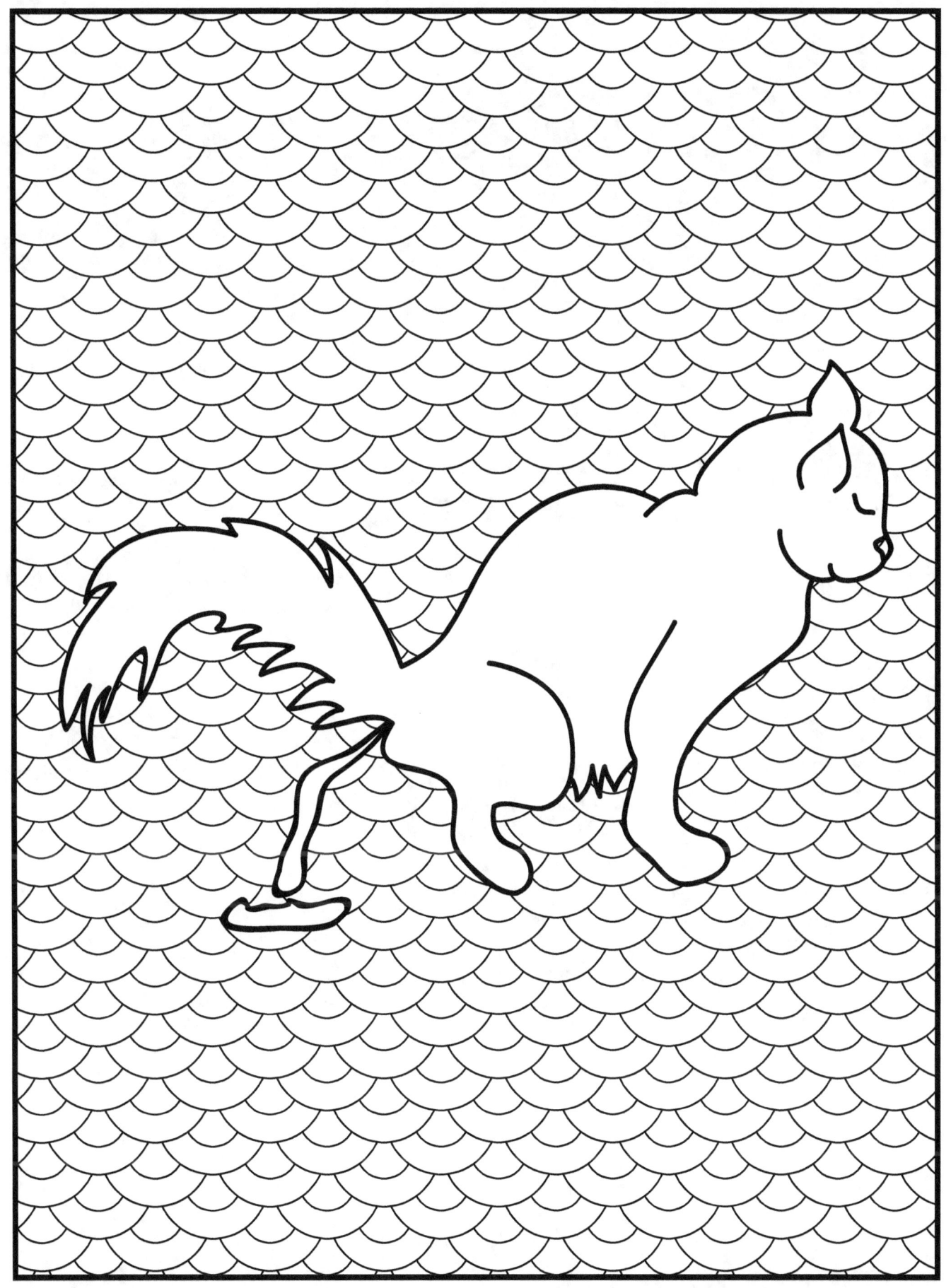

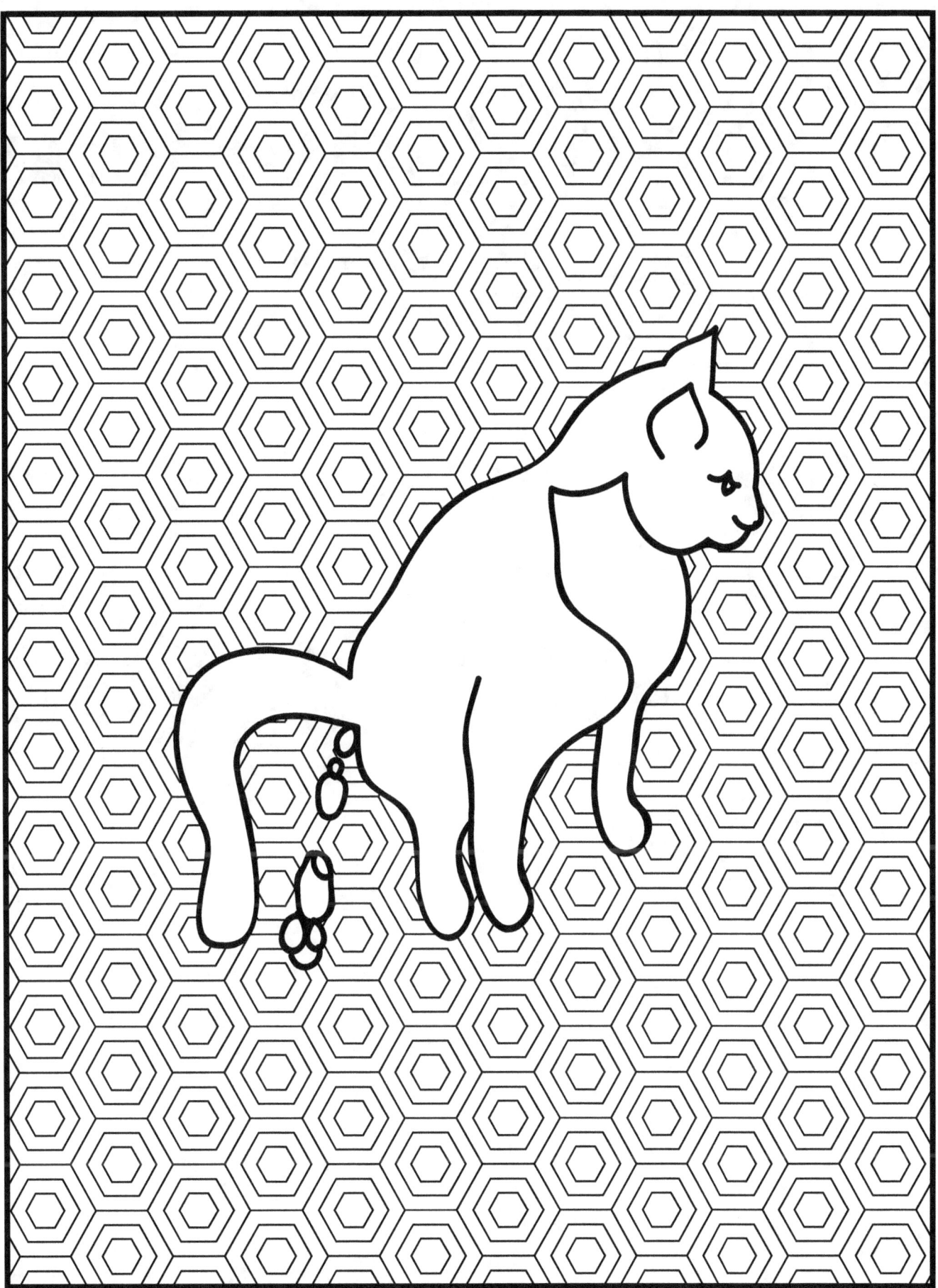

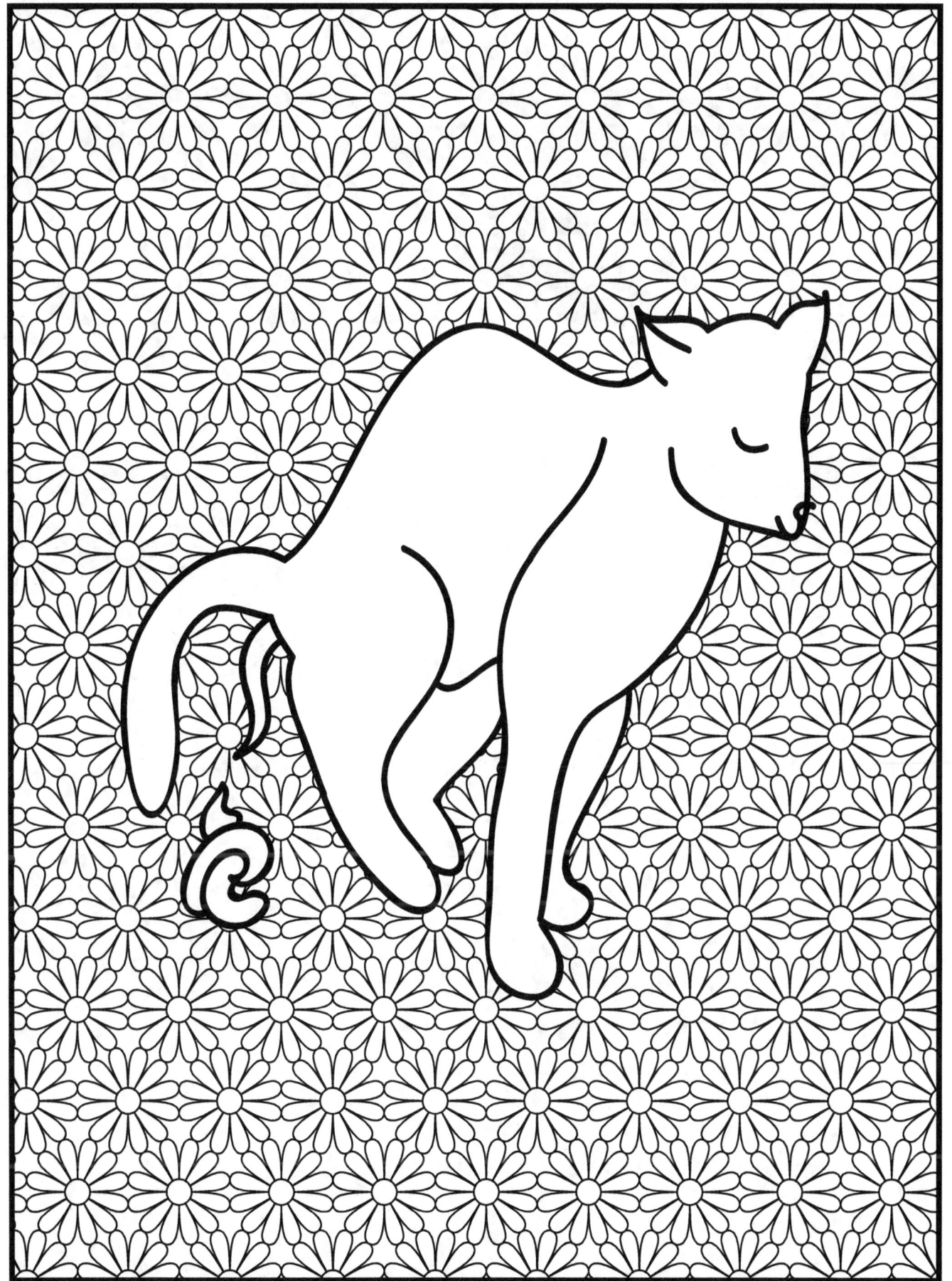

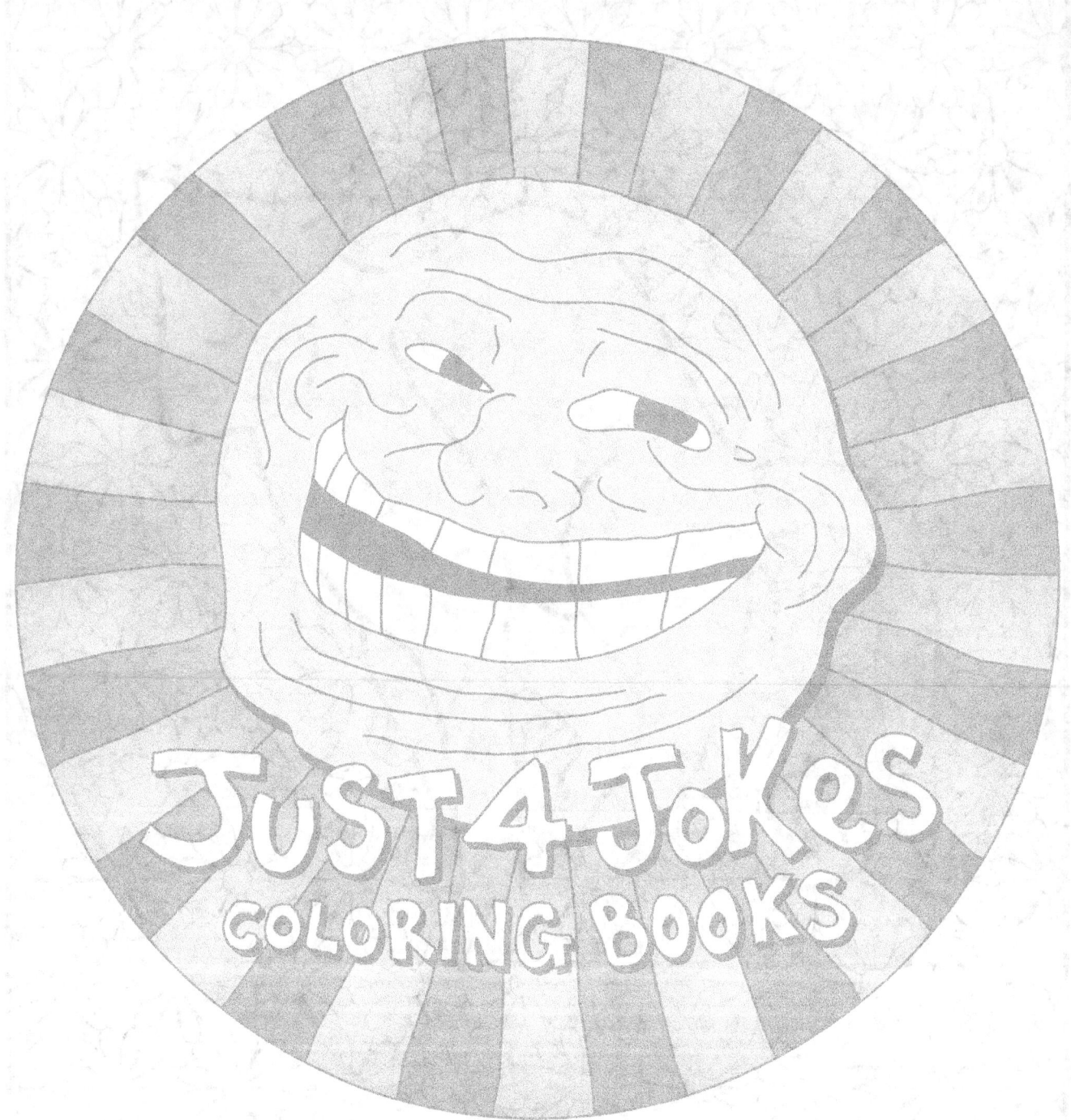

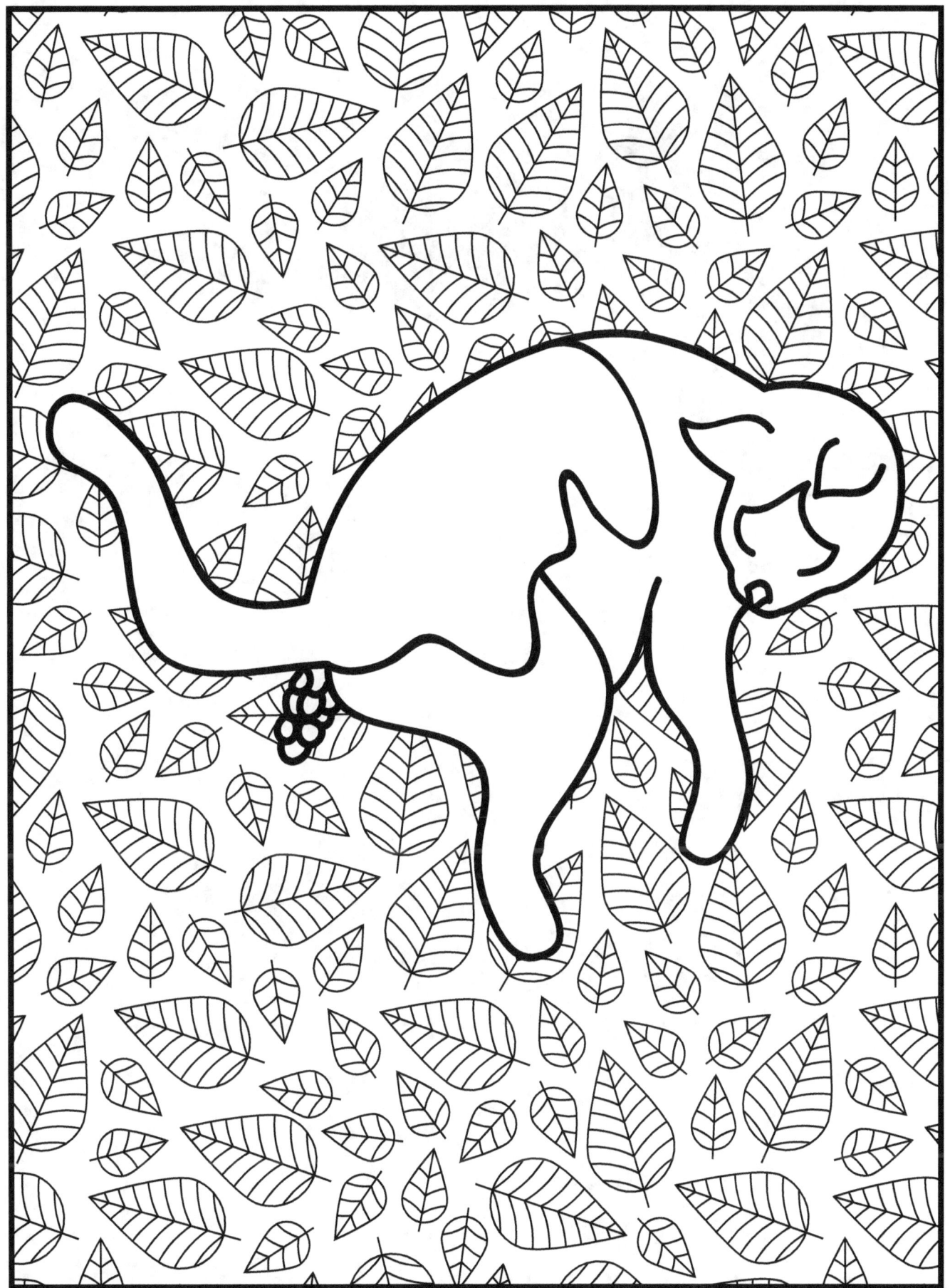

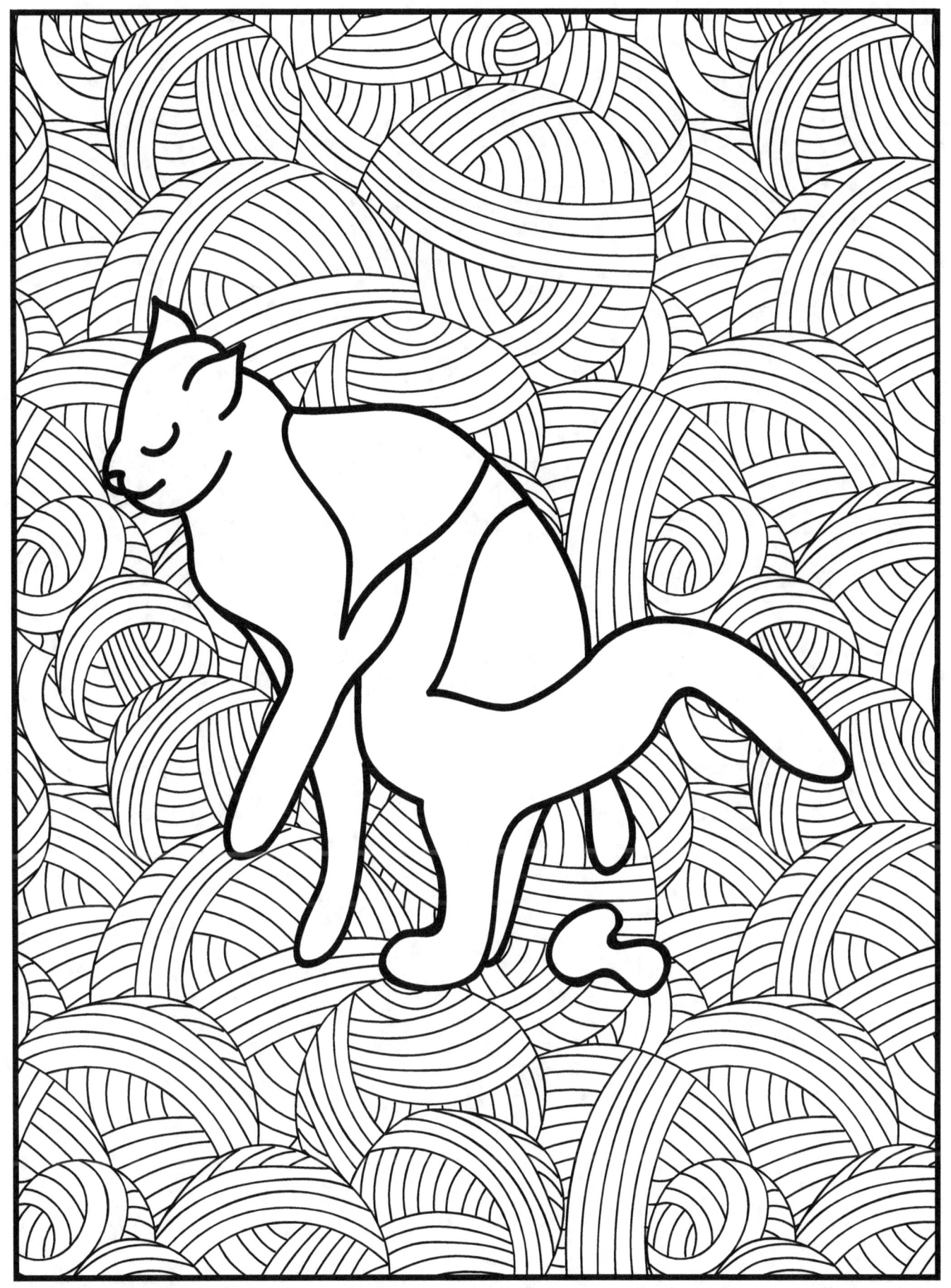

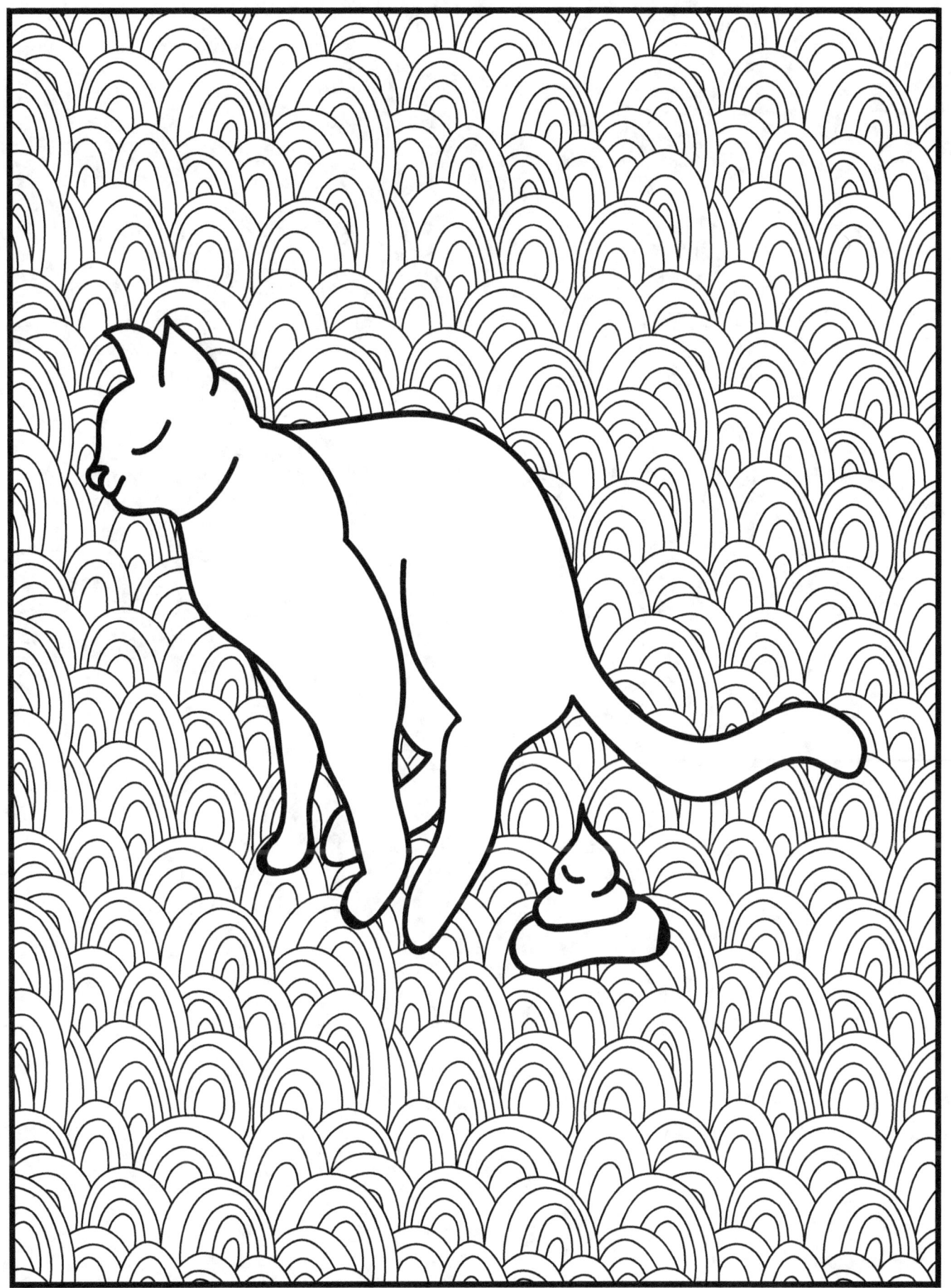

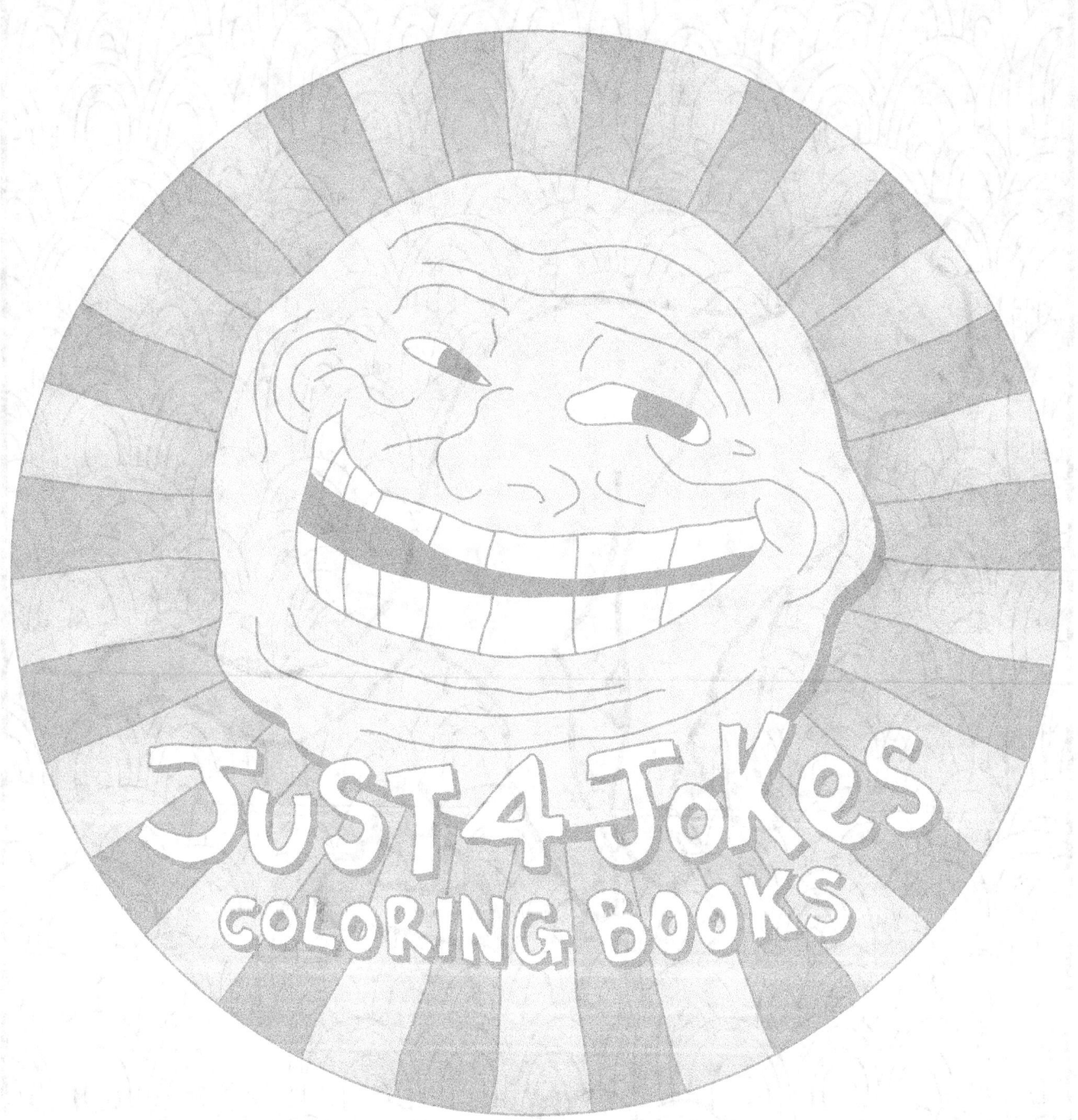

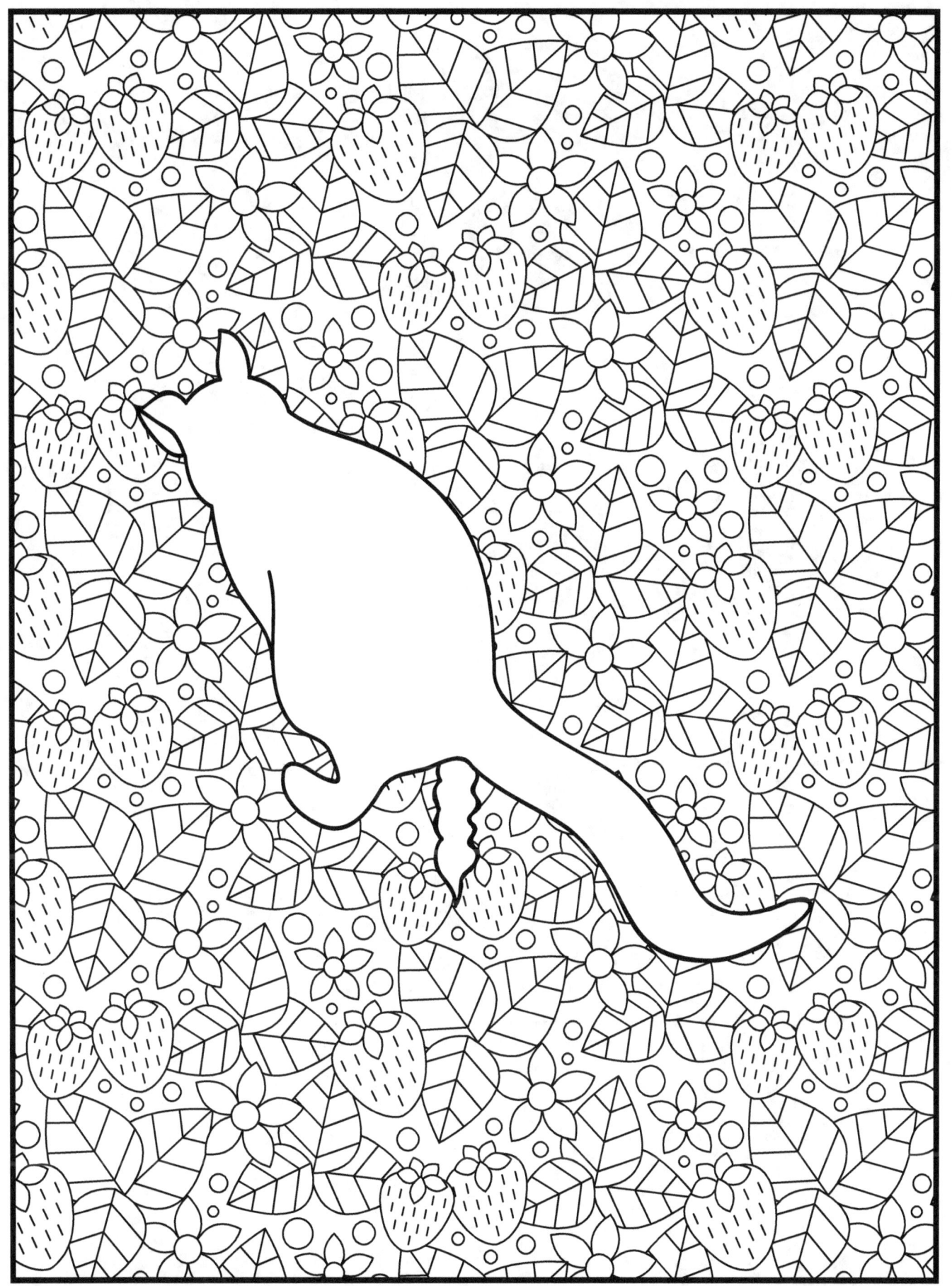

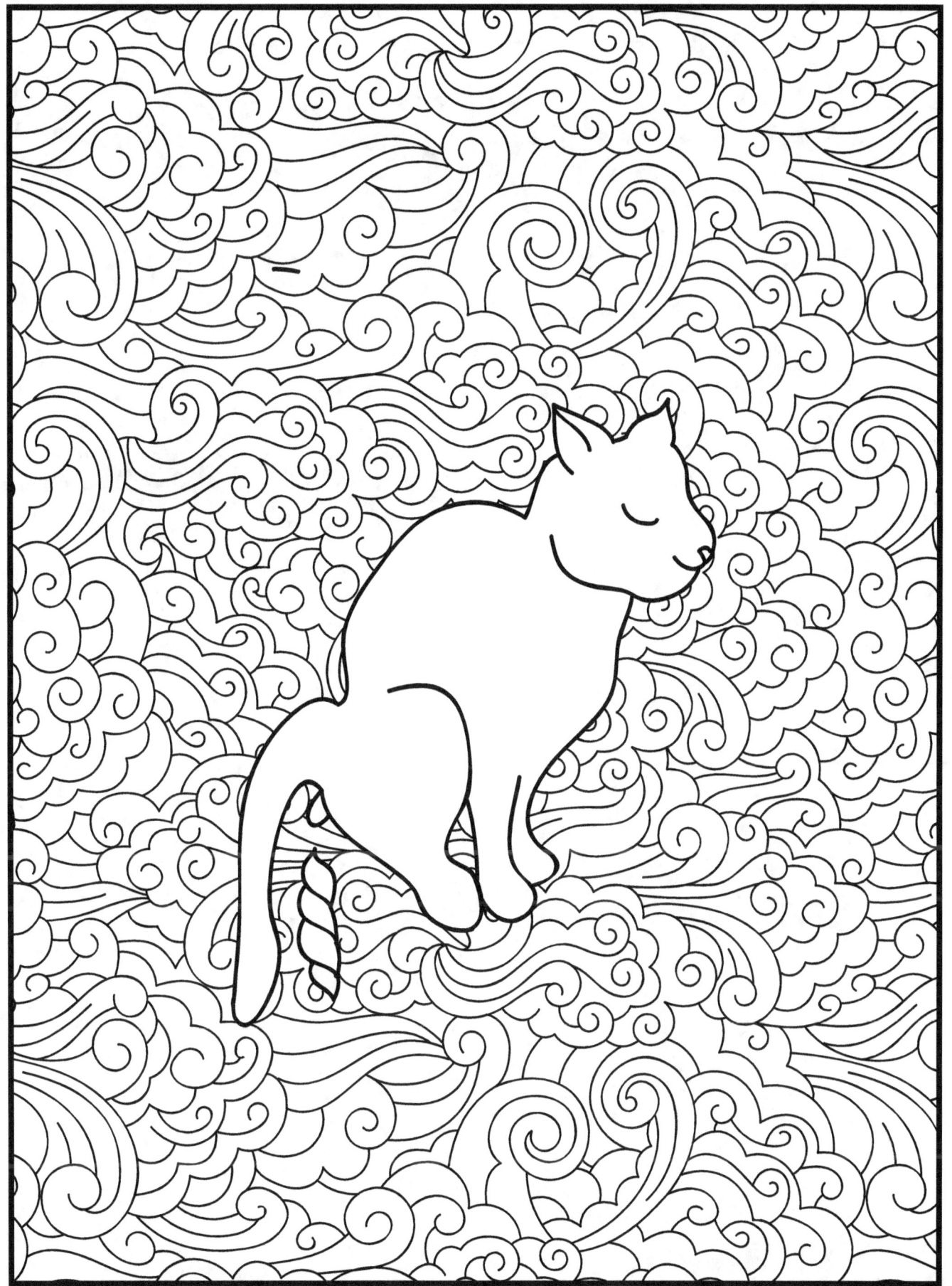

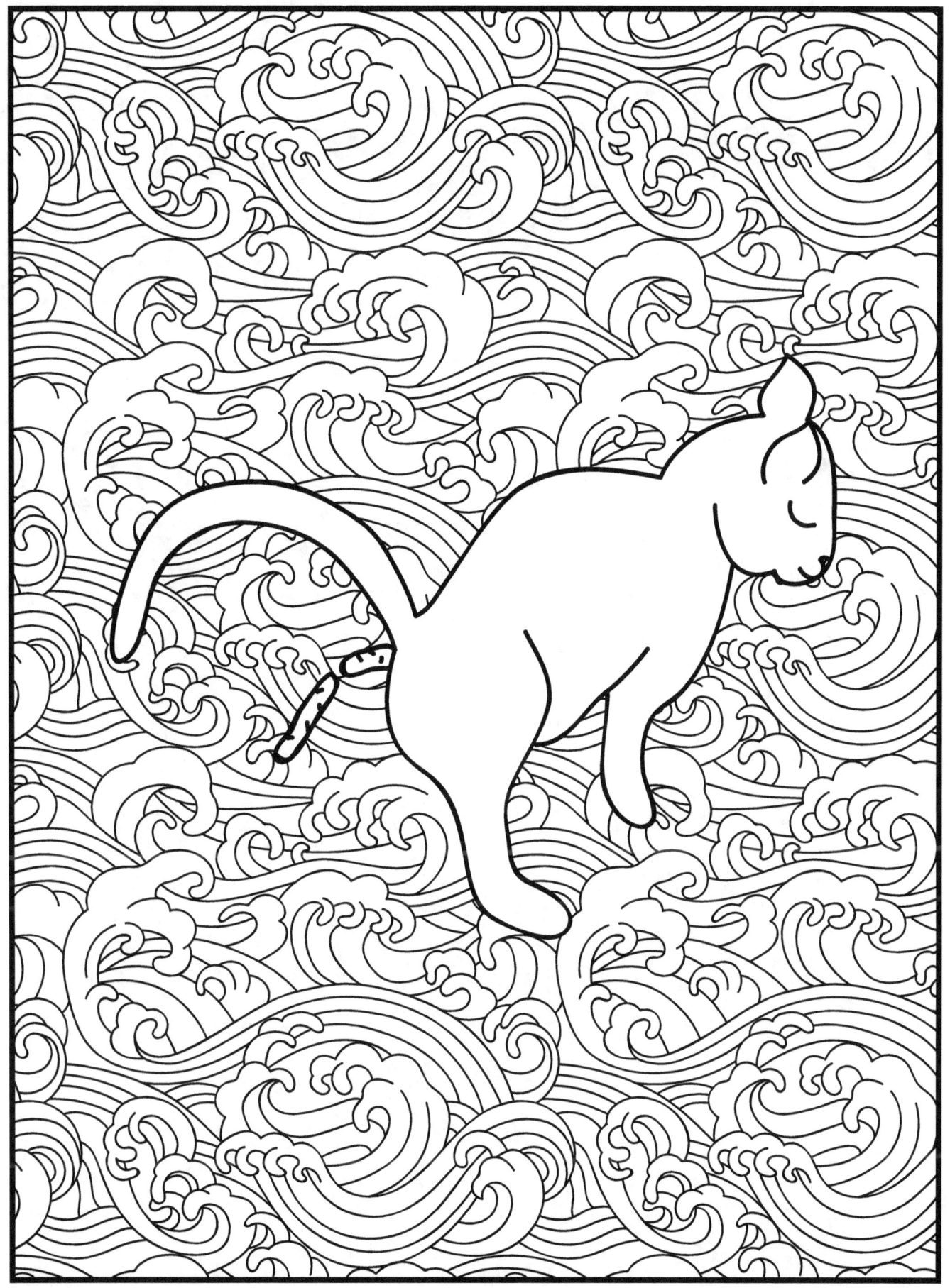

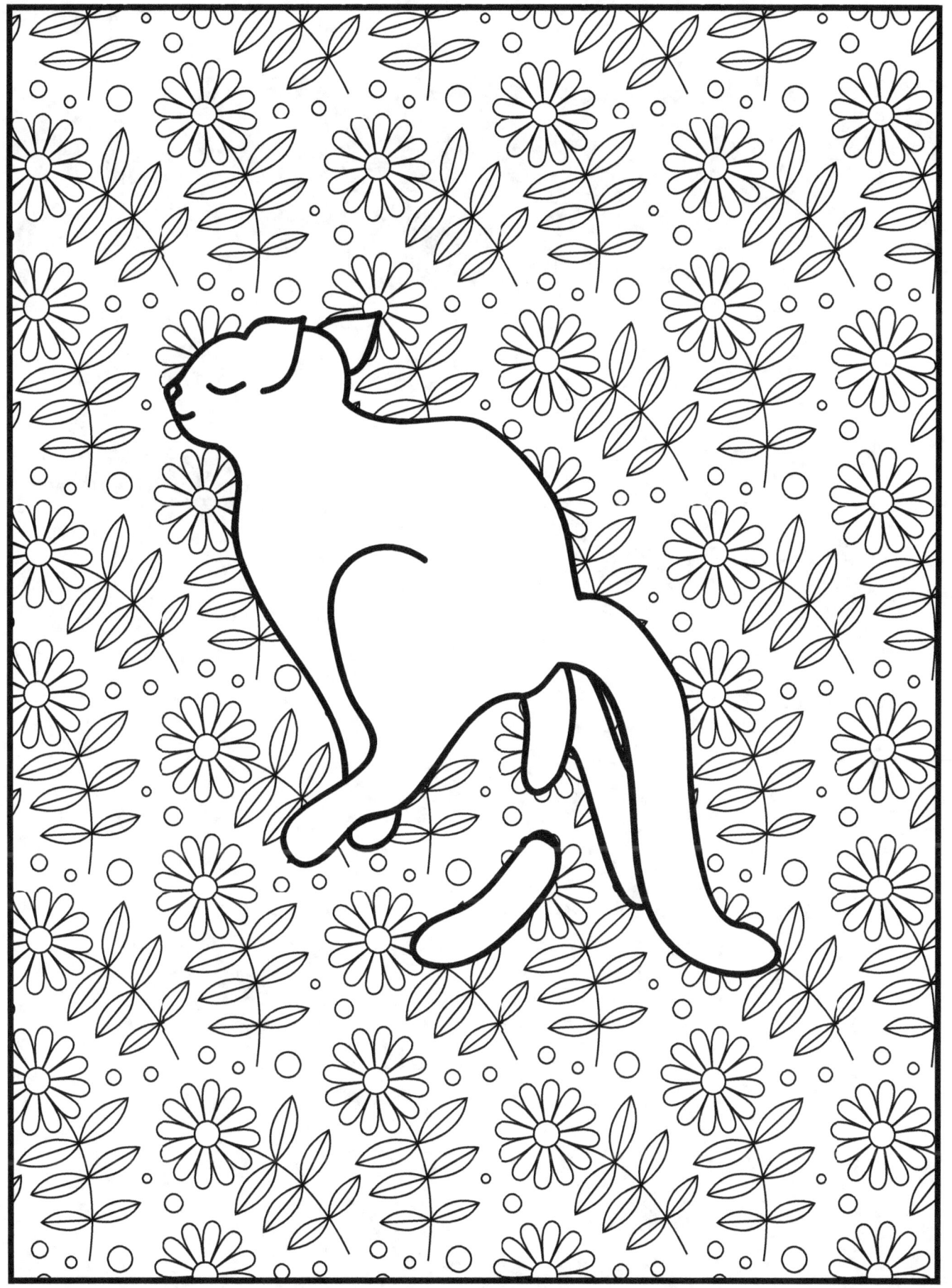

Color Test Page

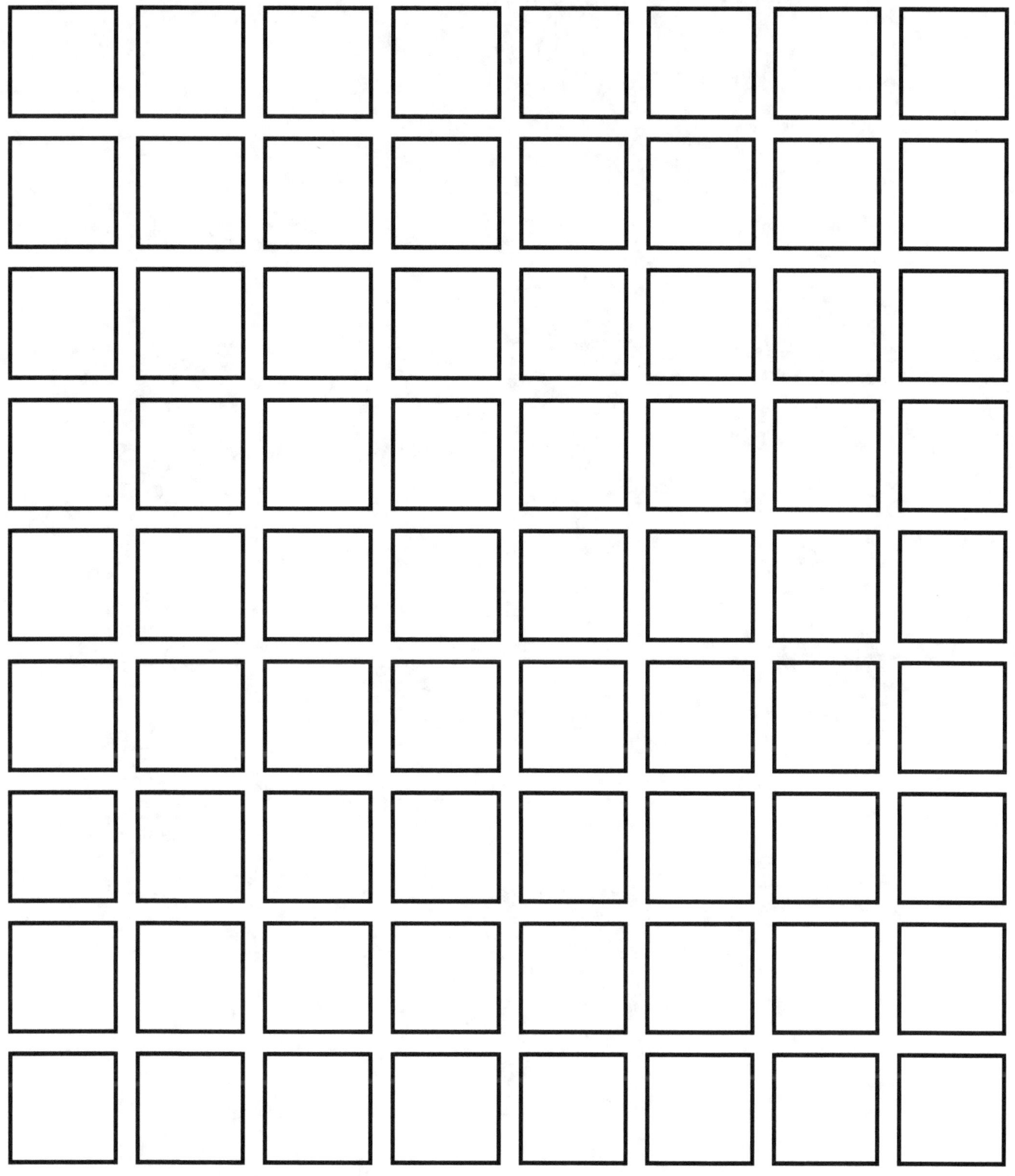

Color Test Page

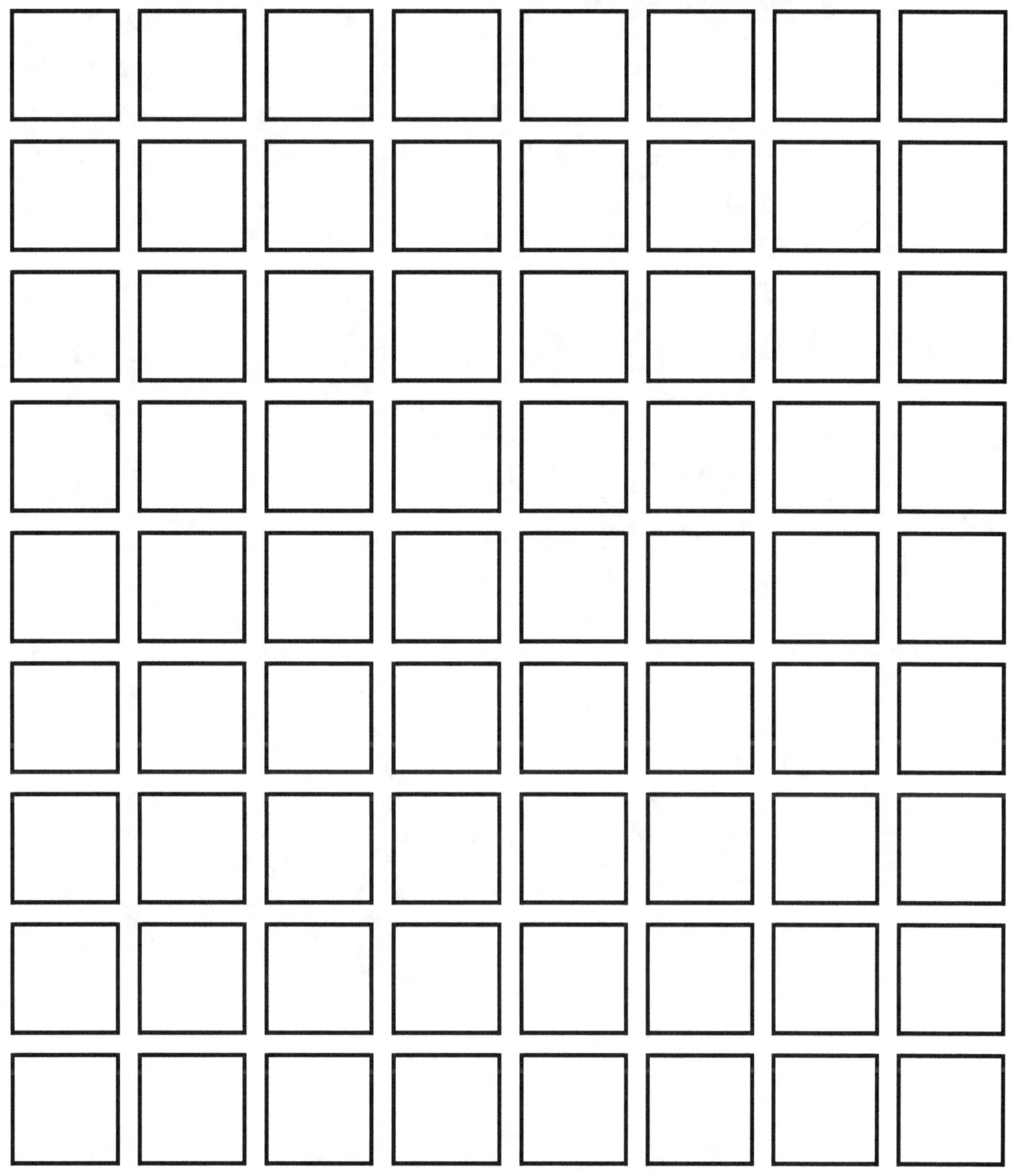

www.ingramcontent.com/pod-product-compliance
Lightning Source LLC
Chambersburg PA
CBHW080816220526
45466CB00011BB/3587